Call Me Not Ishmael but the Sea

Call Me Not Ishmael but the Sea
© J. Martin Daughtry / Cathexis Northwest Press

No part of this book may be reproduced without written permission of the publisher or author, except in reviews and articles.

First Printing: 2023

Paperback ISBN: 978-1-952869-79-2

Cover art by Nora Daughtry, Emily Daughtry, and J. Martin Daughtry
Designed and edited by C. M. Tollefson

Cathexis Northwest Press
cathexisnorthwestpress.com

Call Me Not Ishmael but the Sea

a poem cycle by
J. Martin Daughtry

Cathexis Northwest Press

a la famiglia

Table of Contents

Introduction	1
I / CII: A Bower in the Arsacides	7
II / XL: Midnight 'Forecastle	8
III / XIX: The Prophet	9
IV / CXXVIII: Pequod Meets Rachel	10
V / XCIV: A Squeeze of the Hand	11
VI / CXX: The Deck	12
VII / LVIII: Brit	13
VIII / XX: All Astir	14
IX / CXVI: The Dying Whale	15
X / LXXII: The Monkey Rope	16
XI / XVI: The Ship	18
XII / XLIX: The Hyena	20
XIII / XXIV: The Advocate	21
XIV / CXXV: The Log and Line	22
XV / CXIX: The Candles	24
XVI / LXXXVII: The Grand Armada	26
XVII / XVII: The Ramadan	29
XVIII / XXXI: Queen Mab	30
XIX / CVII: The Carpenter	32
XX / LXXXVI: The Tail	33
XXI / LXIX: The Funeral	35
XXII / CXXXV: The Chase—Third Day	36
XXIII / I: Loomings	38

Introduction

Some years ago—in the earliest stage of an epidemic that was at that time still largely confined to New York City—my family and I left our apartment in Greenwich Village and moved into a small cabin in the Hudson River Valley. We thought we would ride out the crest of the wave of sickness and return to the city in a couple of weeks; we ended up staying there for the better part of a year. It was a strange time, as those of you who lived through it no doubt remember. For me, beyond or beneath the acute fear of microscopic monsters floating in the air lurked a more general feeling of foreboding or dread. This feeling was combined with a hazy sensation that I don't quite have the words to describe. Out there in the country, away from the metropolitan crowds, it seemed (to my anxious, feverishly spinning mind) that the veil of reality that hung over my world was being blown aside to reveal glimpses of a shadowy substance—a queer, flickering spectrality—that I had never experienced before. No, that's not quite right: I *had* experienced this kind of thing before . . . as a very young child who believed in ghosts and magic. At dusk, I saw floating shapes that vanished as soon as I'd squint directly at them. In the middle of the night, I would hear a distant mass of screaming voices (a hyena chorus? I don't think so...) way out in the woods; it would stop instantly as soon as I put my hand on the door knob. Once, on a walk past the small pond down the road, I saw (I am not making this up) the smooth silvery back of some large creature arc up and disappear into the deep. It must have been a turtle, but its color and girth didn't match up with any plausible inhabitant of a pond this size. On these and many other occasions that spring, I felt my grip on what was real and what was imagined (or on what was solid and what was ethereal) slipping. Add to this my constant, grinding fear for my family's health in the face of the illness—not to mention my worryings about the despot in the White House, the looming threat of climate change and mass extinction, and other sources of contemporary gloom and doom—and you can see that I was coming closer and closer to losing it.

During this crazy period, I woke one morning from a literal dream with an idea that made me laugh out loud. (This really happened.) In the dream, I had taken a single chapter from my favorite book, pulled out a few dozen words, and arranged them into a poem. The book is one that I have been reading over and over for twenty-five years, and it, more than any other, has exerted a kind of magic pull over me. I have read it aloud to my young sons, I have read it through on a series of train rides, I have read it in hard copy and on my Kindle and other devices, in all about twelve times. Like many, I first tried (and failed) to read *Moby Dick* in high school; but then I picked it up again as a young man a few years out of college, in the wake of a near-death experience. That autumn, while walking along the Californian coast, I was swept off a rocky promontory by a giant wave. I fell thirty feet into a tide pool, and the withdrawing wave nearly succeeded in pulling me out into the Pacific and certain drowning. I picked up the book on the first day of my convalescence, the first day of the rest of the life I had nearly lost, and was sucked into its dark Oceanica at once. I identified with Pip more than Ishmael—Pip, the humble cabin-boy or "ship-keeper" who too had almost drowned. This is the passage that has haunted me more than any other:

> The sea had jeeringly kept his finite body up, but drowned the infinite of his soul. Not drowned entirely, though. Rather carried down alive to wondrous depths, where strange shapes of the unwarped primal world glided to and fro before his passive eyes; and the miser-merman, Wisdom, revealed his hoarded heaps; and among the joyous, heartless, ever-juvenile eternities, Pip saw the multitudinous, God-omnipresent, coral insects, that out of the firmament of waters heaved the colossal orbs. He saw God's foot upon the treadle of the loom, and spoke it; and therefore his shipmates called him mad. So man's insanity is heaven's sense; and wandering from all mortal reason, man comes at last to that celestial thought, which, to reason, is absurd and frantic; and weal or woe, feels then uncompromised, indifferent as his God.

Over the years, when metaphysical questions arose in my life, I often found myself thinking about this passage, and about Pip, and about the inscrutable whale, and the boundless sea contained by the book's covers. Needless to say, our current unhinged, world-shivering period has caused metaphysical questions to come rattling forward at every turn. With this in mind, it was no surprise that *Moby Dick* should bubble up from my unconscious as I slept. With the excitement of having a new plan throbbing in my head, I attempted, the morning after the dream, to shuffle some of the words from Chapter 102 of *Moby Dick* into a poem that explained what I was hoping to do. I selected that particular chapter because it was the only one in the book that uses the word "poem." "I am composing a poem," I wrote, "Using only words found / In a single chapter of…" and there I wanted to write "*Moby Dick*," or "the book," but neither "Moby Dick" nor the word "book" were present in Chapter 102, so I had to write "the vast word carpet" instead. In the next line I wanted to write something about the author who wrote this particular book/carpet, but "author" wasn't in the chapter either, so I had to opt for "weaver," and "wrote" wasn't available (nor was "weave"), so I had to use the word "tattooed." And so, the first of the stanzas came out like this:

> I am composing a poem
> Using only words found
> In a single chapter of
> The vast word carpet
> That the Leviathanic weaver
> Long ago tattooed
> On the page.

Often, in the ensuing days and weeks, when I had a clear idea about how a line should sound or look, the words I wanted weren't present in a given chapter, so I had to find some kind of substitute. These invariably pleased me more than the word I was searching for ever could have.

Moving forward, I set up strict rules for myself. I could only use the words in a single chapter. The title of each poem would be identical to the title of the chapter it was taken from. If two words were right next to each other, I had to split them up. I was in control of word order and line breaks and periods and question marks and the like, and I could make a lower-case letter capital if I needed to. Otherwise, I could make no changes. I couldn't add a single word of my own; every word had to be written by Melville, and every word had to be found in the chapter I chose.

After the first poem, which I wrote with a specific theme in mind, I tried to approach each new one without a concrete plan. I selected a chapter at random. Then I read it, slowly, a few times, and thought about it a little, after which I began pulling out words that caught my eye and moving them around until they began to feel like they were in the right place. From the beginning, I found that this activity becalmed my troubled mind. Amid the monotonous bark of the news, the nineteenth-century lexicon of *Moby Dick* felt luxurious. The hours and days spent inside a chapter, inside the rich language of the author, felt like medicine. It felt particularly soothing to be freed from the burden of coming up with my own idea for a poem. I loved the slow stirring of the pot until an idea floated up and broke the surface.

The eventual identity of each poem often surprised me. Very few of them lined up in any discernible way with the story of Ahab's monomaniac quest to kill the white whale. Some felt like small philosophical reflections on being and time. Some were abstract, their meaning and even their structure a mystery to me. A few appeared to be about the end of the world. A few appeared to be about love. More than one of them ended up sounding like an inhuman lament, like something written from the perspective of the ocean itself. Regardless, each new construct felt like a little life-buoy bobbing along, keeping me afloat. I was enjoying myself so much that I considered the possibility of arranging one poem for each of *Moby Dick's* 135 chapters—but one of my friends convinced me that literally no one would read that many. I have limited myself to the more modest number of 23. This, as it happens, is the approximate number of threads in a three-inch nautical rope, and it is the number of tiny crossed pairs within the intertwisting hereditary material in every human cell. (Perhaps this is why some of the words on these pages form weaving, intertangled shapes.)

I imagine some of you already suspect—and correctly—that every word of this introduction is *his* as well—every word pulled not from my head but from his book about the whale, every word of his sliding around on my page here like so many slippery slabs of blubber on the deck, until I shuffle them into piles to be rendered in the try-pot, boiled down into ink, as it were. That's right: as with the collection to follow, none of the words of this introduction are mine.[1] But are any words truly ours in the end? Maybe this volume amounts to nothing more than an extreme version of the way words transform themselves whenever they are read? I suppose all books contain an infinity of hidden ghost poems such as these...

In any case, the awkwardness of this introduction is (at least in part) the result of my attempt to bend his words to my particular purpose. But what is this purpose, and is it mine alone? And who am I, here, really? In the end, do "I" even exist? Perhaps, but not here, not fully, not as the sovereign captain of this text. In the strange word maelstrom that follows, "I" am already sinking out of view; or rather, like Pip, or like a ghost, I was only half present in the first place. The only things that are fully here on these pages are the words "tattooed" by the "weaver," whoever that is—along with the gentle pull of the sea, and the cloud-scud blowing off to leeward, and the faint image of the Leviathan breaching near the horizon...

---

[1] While each of the pieces that follow limits itself to the words in a single chapter, this introduction uses words from throughout *Moby Dick*.

I / CII: A Bower in the Arsacides

I am composing a poem
Using only words found
In a single chapter of
The vast word carpet
That the Leviathanic weaver
Long ago tattooed
On the page.

Its warp and woof
Are harpoons and lances
And the skeleton of a certain
White Whale.

Its wondrous woven figures
Its hieroglyphics
Measure life, death
Bursting villainies, humming marvels
Mortal, god
A thousand voices!

I shall not speak the weaver's name.
You know who it is.

II / XL: Midnight 'Forecastle

Plunge into this grand word storm.

Taste the sea-salt in your mouth.
Feel the whale, lurid-like,

Pound and pound away under your floor.

Crish, crash! Blang-whang!
Let us dance to this roaring music and

Rattle the halyards of the gods.

III / XIX: The Prophet

The leg!
The heart!
The head!
Wonderments, all.
They thunder
And laugh
And growl
When shipped upon the waters—
Only half-hinting at
The ineffable stranger
The troubled soul
Broken loose from the vessel of the sailor
Shrouded in ragged reverie
The thought of the parmacetti dogging it
Dogging it
All the way down
Down into the black calabash of night.

IV / CXXVIII: Pequod Meets Rachel

wind — joy

diminished

whale — voice

descending

hull — alarm

drowned

commander — procedure

absent

touch — reason

quivering

search — relent

forgive

V / XCIV: A Squeeze of the Hand

From the try-works to the deck
From the blubber-room to the foremast
Squeezing gently the Leviathan's slobgollion and
His nippers

You serpentine your way up

Up to the
Wondrously oozy decanting
Of that convivial paradise:

The serenely bestreakéd sky.

VI / CXX: The Deck

        Half-stranded
        Masts smack
        Keels and
          Cowards lash
        To the
          Sky-sail of
        Hooroosh
        The Tempest

     …

Everything
  Rises

    Gluepots
      Brain-trucks
       Table-lands
         Cloud-scud

And the
Wildest
Winds are
Medicine
To the
  Anchors

VII / LVIII: Brit

The voyage has been long.
We sluggishly advance through strange fields of
Marshy awfulness, while
Savage sharks glide seethingly by.
The endless foe surrounds us*   [*landsmen, mortals all]
But they will not attack.
They will not crack
the ships and murder
the crews.

Not yet.

***

Do you not sense
        The elephant soundings of the blackened sea
        The accursed flood waters, never to subside
        The future horrors that science renders
        The fiend slowly steering the frigate to doom?
But also
        The terra incognita of ocean plains
        The vast subtleness of a recumbent meadow
        The sagacious tigress hunting on her verdant isle
        The numberless emotions of the whale?

***

This world is not an analogy for all other azure alien worlds.

VIII / XX: All Astir

There is no consolation.
She was not there.
Not in the pantry, not in the rigging.
The woman was not aboard.
Nor was she ashore.
This heaviest thought coils
Down to the ship's hold, where
Absolute and indefatigable
It is roaring
Roaring
Roaring
Like destruction
Upon the fishery.

IX / CXVI: The Dying Whale

wondrousness

turned

worships

infidel

sunward

hushed

speakest

bones

unspoken

faithful

calm

oh!

oh

once

look!

almost

close

floating

water-locked

billows

breaths

rainbowed

beneath

unverdured

dying

nature

all

oh

darker

fire

inwreathing

again

observable

speechless

typhoon

buoyed

curled

thou

unnameable

human

rocks

corpse

a

dark

whale

we

sea

crimson

woe

queen

born

conveyed

water

wild

hum

beneath

exhaled

drowned

O

darker

rolled

earth

X / LXXII: The Monkey Rope

After
Amputating the whale's head, the
Bowsman is sliding in
Blood.
Blood-muddled are we all, and
Blood-shot, for the
Blubber-hook
Breathes
Carnivorous. Its
Chains are
Clumsy but strong. The sea

Devil has
Exposed you to his medicine. He has
Flourished in this world, with its
Great,
Half-drowned
Injustice,
Inseparable from our current

Interregnum.
Involuntarily we fall into
Jeopardy and
Kindle
Lucifer again. His

Massacre of the harpooneers has
Metaphysically imperiled us. Shall
Misfortune ever remain on the sea?
Nearer to the spirits, the
Organ-boys are all
Overboard. They are in
Peril, as are we, as they
Plunge down into the
Poison of this place.

Precious
Queequeg!
Reach down into your
Slacked and
Slaughtered
Spirits, and
Swell up from them a
Trembling happiness,
United by your
Unsounded
Vigilance! The

Waves will not
Wound your inseparable friend
Yojo. His eyes look on with
Zeal.

XI / XVI: The Ship

How is it that
each word, each plank
of this sea-going
vessel was here so
long before me?

And who am I
to set them down
in loose-laced slabs
like so much fresh
cut whale flesh? Who
am I to hear
as poetical
these fibres cut
from the boundless
pilot-cloth?

What ancient creature
forecast these thoughts?
Was it the grim
authority who built this
weather-stained world?
Or was it the old Pequod herself
sailing calmly upon the ocean
before the first man came on board
wriggling her wrinkled wake into
these peculiar Scriptures?

How is a new island formed
in the vagueness of the sea?
How does a ship take its
shape from ivory waves
and whale flukes?
Who stocks the hold?
What hand holds the tiller?
What audacious stillness lives
beneath the flood-tide
of our language?

It is a mystery that dogs more than this volume.

XII / XLIX: The Hyena

You are my disaster
My wayward mate
My fishery, my squall
My leaking heart
My capsizings—
The whales come when you call.

XIII / XXIV: The Advocate

         unpoetical   emulation
          homage   anxiety
          adoration   ridiculous
          honoring   hushed
           vocation   defilements
            freely   earth
             plant   plaudits
              slippery   delights
               recoil   apparition
                politely   consuming
                  harvest   puissant
                    peaceful cosmopolite
                   potentially
                     begotten
                   aggregate
                    womb
               endless unspeakable
             heathenish glory
              ferreting   ah!
             catalogue   oh!
                ailed   blunder-born
           pestiferously   shunned
                 saved   benevolent
                 luckily   declare
             profoundest   terrors
                darting   ancestress
              afterwards   royal
                triumphs   ascribe
            all-abounding   whale

XIV / CXXV: The Log and Line

Oh luckless world!
What oath can mend thee?

Long before now, some
Crazy old captain seized
Nature's immortal quadrant
And hit the rivet on
Its magnet coil
Projecting out a call
Like a mad bell:

                    Ding—dong—ding!

His ship almost breaking
With this energy, the captain
Did not see
The long log-line of horrors
Get heaved—we know not by whom—
overboard.
Thunder rolled through the bulwarks
And all the heavens jumped
Plungingly down
Into the velvet sea.

Man, oblivious, was unmanned.
And now no grey Ahab
Or Manxman

Or Tahitian
Or blind Emperor's idiot
Or golden-hued gods
Can get hold of the
Whirling warped line
That turns and turns
Unwinding you.
And all the while
Till the end of time
The omniscient quadrant
scolds:
                            Ding
                            Dong
                            Ding!

XV / CXIX: The Candles

(To be sung...)

[Starbuck:]
What ceaseless song
The sailors raised
In rolling, rattling power
While sacramental
Skeletons
Fell seething to the sea!

The Ocean was
Indifferent to
The madman and the coward
And unsuffusing
Darkness was
Its own eternity.

> [The crew, jolly, singing:]
> *"Magnanimous, magnanimous*
> *We thunder love upon the whale*
> *Though perilous, so perilous*
> *No fury greater than our gale."*

[Stubb:]
The mariner
With sulfurous breath
Soliloquized the wind:

"I'll worship thee!
Now carry me
On to a sleepy shore."

The heedless air,
Omnipotent,
Raged on till all were blind
Yet still they held
Their song aloft
Effulgent as before:

> [The crew sings defyingly:]
> *"Conspicuous, conspicuous*
> *Our voice leaps upward to the skies.*
> *Though mutinous, aye, mutinous*
> *Thou knowest all our oaths are lies.*
>
> [lower, shrinking, as if overboard]
> *Magnanimous, magnanimous*
> *We thunder love upon the whale*
> *Though perilous, so perilous*
> *No fury greater than our gale..."*

XVI / LXXXVII: The Grand Armada

Indian Ocean.
Some where off the Straits of Sunda.
Black of night.
No wind.
Dead calm.
Hot.

We are eternal months at sea.
Our heads swell at the
Inexhaustible empire of
Concentric circles
the ship draws.

Hours pass.
Then more.
Then, quietly
A vast number of
Transparent
Watery creatures
Come spiralling up
Over the gunwales
And into the ship.
They are floating, snuffling
Touching us!
Their becharmed
Vapors surround the crew
Like a reminiscence

Of sweet cinnamon
Or the all-grasping thought
Of joy.

A deep hum escapes from
one of the creatures.
Far overboard
A whale answers.
His call is even deeper.

Deeper still
Is the singular voice
Of the Universal
Throb, that inscrutable
Body that lurks in the
Serene calm of the ocean's
Deep vault.
We hear it:
Unearthly
        subtle
                endless
                        wondrous.

***

Afterwards, one of the harpooneers admitted:
"We hailed that sea monster.
It rose to the surface.
And so we killed it.

At this the watery
Creatures on the deck all
Vanished into mist.
No more spices.
No more satin-like touching.
They were (we learned)
Entangled with the big one.
This whole turn made
Queequeg quite delirious."

***

In the unimaginable madness of our time
This does not seem at all strange.

XVII / XVII: The Ramadan

   Softly!
      Strange
         Clapping...

            La! La!
               Unaccountable
                  Door...

                     Pry the key-hole to
                  Glimpse the
               Silent Halibut:
                   Heaven's most cheerful
                  Ghost!

XVIII / XXXI: Queen Mab

A queer thing:

In a dream
I tried to speak

To the wind
As it kicked up round
The mast-head.

It did not thunder back
In glory. It didn't
Drop a wise joke
About a merman.

No. It turned

Into a great living
Hump of seaweed
Dragging through
My lungs.

From down in there
It said something
A devilish muttering

About something
Curious I can't now

Remember.

XIX / CVII: The Carpenter

and what of the grand
abstraction?
the quicksilver
unintelligence that
precisely and unhesitatingly
oozed out of
this capricious
half-horrible
world?

there was no
grizzled carpenter
sultanically furnishing
mankind with reference

only the all-ramifying
life-principle
rolling on alone
causelessly inserting
all that matters
into the
outbranching heartlessness
of time

thus is the vermillion plumage of the infinite
awake in the most humble clinging of moss

XX / LXXXVI: The Tail

        curling in
          crescentic
           beauty

                vibrating with
                  a subtle elasticity of
                  grace and playful
                strangeness

          you
          are my
         profoundest
        magic

have you not heard me
           wanting only to express —
   for a —
             bursting to —
  in that moment —
                  — for you?

  appalling!
  nothing comes out

the whale's flukes say it with
a mighty breach
a thunderous smiting of the water

but I can say it only with silence:

> *no one*
> *in all the sea*
> *or world*
> *has such*
> *sweeping*
> *gentleness and*
> *strength*
> *as you*

XXI / LXIX: The Funeral

Insatiate air, stationary
above murderous azure
of water. Further astern,
floating ghosts, lost on the shoal
slowly splash. The sea
flashes with more
and more ghosts
swarming round, like sharks,
though unharming
the marble white fowls
whose obstinate din
hovers
above the spray.

Are they ghosts
or speckled sea-vultures?
Is this the sea
or a vast sepulchre?

XXII / CXXXV: The Chase—Third Day

"The morning of the third day dawned fair and fresh…"
"…a fairer day could not dawn upon that world."
"…there's something all glorious and gracious in the wind…"
"There's a soft shower to leeward."
"'The whale! The ship!' cried the cringing oarsmen."
"…the great shroud of the sea rolled on as it rolled five thousand years ago."

Ahab: Oh, life! Where—and what—were thee?
My mate? My captain? The Pequod animate?
Or might thee have been the whale
That did with such audacity kill me?
No, it is clear now. You were the air itself.
I saw thee not.
Or if I saw, I did so misdoubt thee
In my infallible malice and grief
That, voicelessly, I turned away from thee
Instead of gulping
Thy quivering mist and weather.

Were it not too late I would see thee now
And thrill at thy winds and churning
But I am not here
I am no where, no when.
I am eternal minus.
(As I once said, "*Thus*, I give up the spear.")

All the same
There is a coolness, a calmness
In this much nothing.
I take it in
Steadily
And all grows dim.

XXIII / I: Loomings

Long before the Manhattoes plunged
Towards the barbarous
I formed myself
Conscious, insular
Free of meaning
Bathed in time.

Now horror everlasting
Has come to visit.
Yet I am still a wild wonder-world
Ungraspable by mortal men.

Had I feelings
I would abominate you all.
But I feel nothing.
I am silent
Endless
Invisible.

Call me not Ishmael but
The Sea.

Deep thanks to Emily, Ben, Joey, and Nora Daughtry, who are the primary audience and inspiration for these poems. Thanks too to C. M. Tollefson, the *Cathexis* staff, and everyone who read and commented on early drafts, especially Mike Beckerman, Una Chaudhuri, Sheila Cowley, Patrick Deer, Stuart Goldberg, Robin Preiss, Joel Rust, Sukhdev Sandhu, Lytle Shaw, Johannes Snape, and Cristina Vatulescu. My most profound gratitude is reserved for Herman Melville, and for the whales and oceans that haunted his dreams.

J. Martin Daughtry is an associate professor of music and sound studies at New York University, where he teaches courses on the subjects of acoustic violence; human and nonhuman voices; listening and non-listening; sound and environment; the auditory imagination; and jazz. He is the author of *Listening to War: Sound, Music, Trauma, and Survival in Wartime Iraq* (Oxford University Press, 2015); and is a founding curator of the Analogue Humanities Archive and Symposium, an enigmatic organization that, by design, has no internet footprint. His most recent literary essay, "Florida, Farewell," was published in *AGNI* in 2022.

Also Available from Cathexis Northwest Press:

Something To Cry About
by Robert Krantz

Suburban Hermeneutics
by Ian Cappelli

God's Love Is Very Busy
by David Seung

that one time we were almost people
by Christian Czaniecki

Fever Dream/Take Heart
by Valyntina Grenier

The Book of Night & Waking
by Clif Mason

Dead Birds of New Zealand
by Christian Czaniecki

The Weathering of Igneous Rockforms in High-Altitude Riparian Environments
by John Belk

If A Fish
by George Burns

How to Draw a Blank
by Collin Van Son

En Route
by Jesse Wolfe

sky bright psalms
by Temple Cone

Moonbird
by Henry G. Stanton

southern athiest, oh, honey
by d. e. fulford

Bruises, Birthmarks & Other Calamities
by Nadine Klassen

Wanted: Comedy, Addicts
by AR Dugan

They Curve Like Snakes
by David Alexander McFarland

the catalog of daily fears
by Beth Dufford

Shops Close Too Early
by Josh Feit

Vanity Unfair and Other Poems
by Robert Eugene Rubino

Destructive Heresies
by Milo E. Gorgevska

Bodies of Separation
by Chim Sher Ting

The Night with James Dean and Other Prose Poems
by Allison A. deFreese

About Time
by Julie Benesh

The Unempty Spaces Between
by Louis Efron

SUSPENDED
by Ellen White Rook

Coming To Terms
by Peter Sagnella

Cathexis Northwest Press

www.ingramcontent.com/pod-product-compliance
Lightning Source LLC
Chambersburg PA
CBHW082027120526
44592CB00039B/2624